D1559669

RICH BY 22

*HOW TO ACHIEVE BUSINESS SUCCESS
AT AN EARLY AGE*

Tom Corson-Knowles

**Copyright © 2012, 2013, 2014
by Tom Corson-Knowles**

**All rights reserved. No part of this book may be
used or reproduced by any means, graphic,
electronic, or mechanical, including photocopying,
recording, taping or by any information storage
retrieval system without the written permission of
the publisher except in the case of brief quotations
embodied in critical articles and reviews.**

ISBN 978-1-6316100-3-5

**To get more free tips and information on how to
you too can achieve business and financial
success in just a few short years, sign up for my
free newsletter at**

www.BlogBusinessSchool.com

Earnings Disclaimer

When addressing financial matters in any of books, sites, videos, newsletters or other content, we've taken every effort to ensure we accurately represent our products and services and their ability to improve your life or grow your business. However, there is no guarantee that you will get any results or earn any money using any of our ideas, tools, strategies or recommendations, and we do not purport any "get rich schemes" in any of our content. Nothing in this book is a promise or guarantee of earnings. Your level of success in attaining similar results is dependent upon a number of factors including your skill, knowledge, ability, dedication, business savvy, network, and financial situation, to name a few. Because these factors differ according to individuals, we cannot and do not guarantee your success, income level, or ability to earn revenue. You alone are responsible for your actions and results in life and business. Any forward-looking statements outlined in this book or on our Sites are simply our opinion and thus are not guarantees or promises for actual performance. It should be clear to you that by law we make no guarantees that you will achieve any results from our ideas or models presented in this book or on our Sites, and we offer no professional legal, medical, psychological or financial advice.

WHY I WROTE THIS BOOK

Did you ever have a dream when you were a kid? Did you dream of becoming an astronaut or firefighter or some other dream career? Well I did! As a kid, I always dreamed that someday, somehow I would be able to live my dream: to be able to do whatever I wanted whenever I wanted wherever I wanted with whomever I wanted to be with.

I guess my dream was more of a "being" thing than a doing thing. I didn't really want to be a doctor or a lawyer or some big shot. I just wanted freedom! I wanted to be free from all the rules and obligations of childhood like going to school, doing what my parents told me to do and staying home. Instead, I wanted complete freedom to do what I wanted. I wanted to travel and visit every country in the world. I wanted to have glorious adventures and not be stuck in school or a job. Have you ever felt like that?

Well, when I was 19 years old in college, I decided I had enough of doing what everyone else wanted me to do.

Fortunately or unfortunately, I didn't have the guts to drop out of school. But I started writing... I started writing down my goals, my dreams and my philosophy on life. I started studying great business leaders and wealthy people who shared how they became so successful. I finally decided then and there that I was either going to build my own business and get rich or die trying!

At that time, I started my manifesto if you will. It was my way of clarifying my beliefs, thoughts, attitudes and activities that I needed to do to get rich and become financially free. At first, the book was just for me. I never planned for anyone else to read it. I found that just in the writing of it, I became inspired, motivated and called to a higher purpose in life. I started a tiny business and that tiny business began to grow... and grow... and grow some more.

Before I knew it, I was so busy with my growing business and schoolwork that I couldn't find time to work on the book! It stayed dusty and deserted on my computer until six years later. When I re-read the book at age 25, I realized that my dream had come true. I had become financially free. I was earning more money every month than I ever dreamed possible! And it was all on autopilot. Some call it "passive income." Even if I quit working today, I couldn't stop the checks from coming!

I also realized that other people needed to hear this message. I knew that if what I wrote in this book was powerful enough to help me become financially free that it could do it for others. So I worked day and night for months editing the book, clarifying the message, honing it down to just the most essential keys for business, financial and personal success in life.

The result is this book – Rich by 22. I know that if a 19 year old shy kid like me can become financially free and retire in 3-5 years that you can too!

Thank you for purchasing my book Rich by 22! I'm wishing you the best of success, happiness, and health in your life.

TABLE OF CONTENTS

INTRODUCTION
IT'S ALL ABOUT YOUR POINT OF VIEW!

YOUR VIEW OF BEING RICH

We all have our own view of what being rich means. And with that view comes our own prejudices, beliefs, notions, feelings, thoughts and habits.

And, of course, it's our actions in life that determine what happen to us. You have choices in life – every single day. To start a business or keep doing what you're doing. To study hard and research or play video games. To work out or watch TV. You always have choices... especially when it comes to getting rich.

Being rich is not what you think it is. And being rich doesn't mean anything.

Richness in and of itself means absolutely nothing. But you make it mean something. Maybe you make it mean people who are rich are bad. Maybe you make it mean being rich will make you happy. Maybe you make it mean being rich will make you shallow. Begin to notice the meaning you have attached to being rich, to money, and to finances in general.

Whatever you make it mean, I invite you to let it go. Just let go of your view of what being rich means. You see, there's no power if you say people who are rich are bad because then you will lose out on the possibilities of relationships with people who happen to be rich. And if your best friend gets rich, you will think he is a bad person because he happens to be rich. How messed up is that?

But people let those little beliefs run their entire lives... and they never realize why they just can't seem to scrape by enough money to do what they REALLY want to do with their lives. Don't let that be you!

Just as there is no power in negative beliefs about being rich, there is no power if you say being rich will make you happy. Because then, no matter what, you will never be happy until you get rich. And I can promise you if you are never happy until you get rich, you won't be happy once you are rich!

You see, you get what you practice in life. If you keep practicing being unhappy all the time, you'll keep being unhappy. Money won't change that – I know because I've been there and done that.

There's no power in making being rich mean you are shallow or vain, because then you will avoid doing the actions and having the feelings of being rich because you don't want to be shallow. Why limit yourself financially?

You've got to realize you will never have power over your financial life unless and until you give up the meanings you have put on objects, situations, and things outside of yourself. You must realize that you are in control of your life, in every way, in every situation, now, in the past, in the future and always.

You are all-powerful. You are a creator. So I invite you to come along with me and create richness and abundance for yourself and for the world. Your life as you know it has just begun anew.

Right now!

CHAPTER 1
BEGIN WITH THE END IN MIND

Have you ever been with someone and asked, "What do you want to do?" and they responded, "I don't know." How lame is that?

These are the kind of people that go through their day like the walking dead. This is the kind of nonchalant attitude you need not accept if you want to be successful. Avoid the quiet, boring march to death and decide what you REALLY want to do with your life!

Now I'm not saying you're a bad person if you don't know what you want to do with your life. All I'm saying is you better spend some time thinking about it instead of watching TV or you'll end up like the other broke people who watch TV all day, wishing they had those nice cars and mansions they always see on VH1.

Every rich person I've ever met had a vision for their life – a calling to do something unique. Some wanted to be artists, actors, entrepreneurs, teachers... they all had a dream. What's your dream?

Society does a good job of suppressing people today. The average child hears no at least 400 times a day!

"You can't do that" is said much too often while "you can do it" has been converted into a cliché slogan which many people ignore. Stop listening to negative people. It is undoubtedly true that if someone else can become rich, you can too. You CAN become rich. Anyone can. It's all about your choices.

Successful people know what they want.

Bob Proctor says:

> *"If you can SHOW me what you want,*
> *I can show you how to get it."*

Why does Bob make this incredible promise? Because it's true! If you actually know what you want and are committed to it, you will get it.

I can show you how to get rich but I can't tell you why you should do what it takes to get rich. Your desire is a key ingredient that can come only from you. You must decide to become rich. You must also decide why you want to become rich.

What are your reasons for achieving great things? Why try that hard? Why get up that early? Why stay up that late? Why live the life of your dreams?

WHY NOT?

History is full of examples of great people who decided what they wanted and made it happen.

Andrew Carnegie wrote on a small note and kept it in his desk over the years a simple message that shows how powerful writing down your intentions and goals really is.

Carnegie wrote:

> *"I will spend the first half of my life making money, and the second half giving it all away."*

And that's exactly what he did. Carnegie gave away over $350 million in his lifetime by the time he died in 1919. That was back when money was money. I mean, $350 million back then is equivalent to more than $10 billion today.

He was the one of the greatest philanthropists in the history of the world. Why? Because he wanted to be. That was his goal. That was his dream.

I'm not saying you should be a philanthropist. Personally, I want to give away hundreds of millions of dollars to worthy causes in my lifetime. But I'm not asking you to adopt MY goals and dreams – all I'm asking is that you find your own.

Be a good student, but don't just be a follower. Learn everything you can but make your own decisions.

Don't try to live someone else's life – this is YOUR LIFE. Make it be what you want it to be. Screw what everyone else thinks. They can plan their own lives – but not yours. Your life is for you to live and you alone. And at the end of the day what you do with it is entirely up to you.

SET THE STANDARD

Roger Bannister was the first man to ever run a mile in under 4 minutes. Well before he ever accomplished this feat, he openly proclaimed that he would do it. He set his mind on it. Roger Bannister was not the most fit or athletic person in the world. He simply *knew* that he wanted to run a mile in less than 4 minutes. And he did.

What's incredible about Bannister's accomplishment is that within nine months *36 other people ran a mile in under 4 minutes.* In the last 5000 years of recorded history, no man had run a mile in under 4 minutes EVER. And then all of sudden nearly 40 people did just that in less than a year.

That is the power of knowing what you want. Today, even some high school students have run a mile in under 4 minutes.

Before Bannister ran the mile in under 4 minutes many people said that a human being was incapable of running that fast. They said your heart would stop if you ran that fast. Maybe people had been saying that for thousands of years. Maybe that's why no one ever ran a mile in under 4 minutes. But all it took was one man to say "I want it and I will do it." That is the power of setting goals and committing to action.

The problem many of us face is we have notes on our desks that say things like, "I need to get diapers for Tommy after I pick up McDonald's for dinner and go to the dry cleaner."

We know how to take care of errands, but have we accomplished something great with our life? Have we made a difference in the world? Are we living up to our real potential? Or are we just settling for an average life?

As Confucius said:

> *"A man who shoots at nothing*
> *is sure to hit it."*

Don't let that be you.

All I'm saying is that I'd rather aim for trillionaire and settle for millionaire than aim for nothing and stay broke all my life. How about you?

Playing Big

I love Donald Trump because he always talks about being big, playing big, and thinking big. It seems like Trump's favorite word is BIG. Donald trump is clearly playing big in life. He has big cars, big boats, big buildings, and a big attitude. He has also made a big difference in millions of peoples' lives through his businesses, writings, books and teachings.

Now I'm not saying I think Trump is a great guy or that I'd like to be his best friend. What I'm saying is he's clearly playing a much bigger game than most of us play. Most of us just worry about how to pay the rent – Trump worries about how to build thousands of apartments for people to lie in. There's a big difference in the impact!

Most people play small. If you want real freedom, power, and joy in life you must learn to play a bigger game. Instead of worrying about how you are going to pay your bills, worry about how you can help others pay their bills. Instead of worrying about your financial security, help others achieve financial security.

While some people are worrying about how they can't afford a car, others are buying the whole dealership!

I highly recommend reading books, watching videos, and listening to recordings of people who play big in life, like Mahatma Gandhi, Martin Luther King, Warren Buffett, Mother Theresa, Chris Gardner, Bill Gates, Steve Jobs, and many more.

Nothing will open your mind up to possibilities like learning from these great people who played big in life and have achieved incredible things - accomplishments that many others had said were impossible.

As Napoleon Hill wrote in *Think and Grow Rich*:

"The real measure of intelligence is action."

So get to work! Set your goals and commit yourself to playing big.

RECOMMENDED READING ON GOALS:

- ➤ *7 Habits Of Highly Effective People* by Stephen Covey
- ➤ *Think and Grow Rich* by Napoleon Hill
- ➤ *4-Hour Work Week* by Tim Ferriss

CHAPTER 2
GROW OR DIE!

There is one simple law in the universe that most people are either unaware of or ignore, to their own detriment. That law is this:

> **"You are either growing or dying –
> there is no middle ground."**

Do you know how scientists find the age of a pine tree? They count the rings of growth.

Each year, the tree grows and creates a new ring of new wood every year without fail. Some years the rings are big and some small, but no matter what a living tree always grows another ring each year.

When a pine tree fails to grow a new ring one year, you know the tree is dead. That's it. There is no middle ground. There are no pine trees that live but decide not to grow. Their nature is to grow or die.

> ***"YOUR nature is to grow or die."***

Likewise, human beings are meant to grow every year. We are meant to grow intellectually, spiritually, emotionally, and in every area of our life. You are either growing or dying.

This law may be easiest to see in the world of business. When you see a business that's growing, it's doing well and everything is great. But when you see a business that fails to grow, you know it is dying.

It's clear to the people inside the business that something is not right. The best employees tend to leave when a business starts dying, and the business usually goes bankrupt or is sold off. Of course we all know of an amazing business turnaround where a floundering business became a thriving, growing company. These turnarounds only happen because someone in the organization decided to grow the business again instead of worrying about maintaining the status quo.

In your life, if you feel like you're floundering, stuck, or just not achieving the success you want, realize that it will only turn around when you decide to start growing again.

I know you are ready to grow because you are reading this book!

CHAPTER 3
DO KARATE YES OR DO KARATE NO

In the movie Karate Kid, Mr. Miyagi says, *"Do Karate yes, or do Karate no"* – there is no "guess so" karate.

This means you have to put your ass on the line. Most people live a "guess so" life. They are afraid (as we all are) and so they live a half-assed life and get less than half the results. Real power comes from being committed to something and never from holding yourself back.

Have you ever heard someone say, "I'll try to do that." Talk about living a half-assed life!

I've never seen someone try. Have you ever seen someone try? I have seen people show up to an educational event, but I have never seen someone trying to show up to an event.

I have seen people do great things, but I have never seen people trying to do great things.

I have seen salespeople make a difference in peoples' lives by selling products but I have never seen a salesperson trying to sell.

Trying is just an excuse we use so we do not have to take responsibility for our own actions, or lack of actions.

If you told your significant other, "Honey, I'm going to try not to cheat on you," how would that go? Probably not well.

Likewise, when you tell people in your life "I'm going to try to show up," you send the wrong message - the message is that you are not committed to what you say. You are living a half-assed life, and everyone knows it. Whether or not people in your life confront you on your bullshit, they all know the truth.

The problem is we all have our own bullshit. We all "let things slide" when we know we shouldn't. It's like everyone is playing a game called "Don't call me out on my shit and I won't call you out on yours."

Trust me, a REAL friend will call you out on your bullshit. They'll tell you when you mess up. Because if you don't learn from your own mistakes you'll just keep making the same ones over and over!

Brian Tracy says, "everyone knows everything." That means, everyone knows how hard you work, or not.

Everyone knows how much time you waste watching TV.

Everyone knows if you skip work early.

Everyone knows if you studied for that test or not.

The good thing is that everyone knows when you do work hard. Everyone knows when you go out of your way to help others. Everyone knows when you commit to something and follow through on your commitments.

Live your life as if everyone is watching your every action – not that you should feel pressured, but because you should be respected for your accomplishments and good actions. You should live a life that you are proud of. Don't hold back!

When you are willing to give up trying and ready to start doing, your life will begin to change dramatically. You will find yourself achieving dramatic results you have never achieved before. You will find yourself being WAY more effective. Others will respect you for your commitment to life.

You will have more self-esteem, more power, more fun, and feel more alive than you ever have before. With commitment comes power – the power to create your own life as you wish it to be – rich, happy, loving and fun.

Chapter 4
Awareness is Key

On September 15, 2008 Lehman Brothers declared bankruptcy. That day was a turning point in the financial world. The game has changed. Are you aware of what is happening today?

Most people keep talking about the recession. They want you to be afraid. While others are busy worrying, the rich are getting richer and the poor are getting poorer. Why? Because the rich people spend their time focusing on gaining awareness of new opportunities while poor people tend to focus on the difficulties and worries.

Despite what you may hear in the news about the economy or finances, today is the easiest time to get rich there has ever been in the history of the world!

Now that is a bold statement. But it's true!

Here are just a few of the reasons why:

Information is more readily available today through the internet to just about anyone, anywhere at anytime

The world stock markets fell between 30-50%, real estate prices have fallen as much as 70% in some areas, and there are more possible investments today than ever before in the history of the world!

The internet has created an opportunity for ANYONE to start an online business for less than $100 – for those who are willing to learn how. (By the way, I teach how to start a business online for beginners and you can learn everything you need to know for free at www.BlogBusinessSchool.com.)

Direct selling is set to be the next trillion dollar industry according to Paul Zane Pilzer, and the investment to start a direct selling business is usually less than $100 while the profit potential is huge. That means anyone can get started in a business for less than $100 AND have someone teach you the entire way through!

There are more millionaires today than ever before

There are more people with spending money on the planet than ever before (which means more potential customers for every business!)

There are more opportunities today than ever before. I know it's commonly said that you must be in the right place at the right time to make it in life. I don't think that's entirely true. You see, you have to be *aware* that you are in the right place at the right time. If you're not aware, then you're going to miss out.

Start becoming more aware of the opportunities all around you. Do you see the opportunities everywhere?

On my daily run a few weeks ago, I saw a yard sale and decided to stop running and check it out. I found books for sale for 25 cents each. I noticed a few books that I knew I could sell for at least $10 on Amazon.com. So I bought the books, resold them on Amazon, and I made a return on my investment of over 4,000%!

Now I know, it was less than $50 in profit - but it only took me 5 minutes. And more importantly, it expanded my awareness of what is possible. I am always looking for new opportunities – and I always find them. Are you looking for opportunities?

Like all things, building your awareness takes practice. That's what I was doing with buying and selling those books – practicing to increase my awareness. I recommend you do the same.

Today, find an opportunity to increase your income and increase your wealth. They're everywhere. All you have to do is look.

Even if you just start with a $5 transaction, so what? That could be the beginning of the next billion-dollar company! After all, McDonald's earns billions of dollars a year selling one $5 meal at a time.

CHAPTER 5
SAY "YES!" TO YOU!

> "Yes is magic and opens hearts – no blocks heart.
>
> Yes improves love life – no destroys love.
>
> Yes opens for direct communication – no ends communication.
>
> Yes opens for direct love and creates flow of love through both – recipient and source of love and YES thus creates happiness! – no separates lovers.
>
> Yes establishes a link of love – no cuts that link.
>
> Yes creates the flow of love needed for healing of body, heart and soul – no stops healing.
>
> Yes creates oneness – no separates.
>
> Yes creates holiness – no creates ego.
>
> Yes creates divinity – no creates destruction and disaster.
>
> Yes creates peace – no creates tension.
>
> Yes is the beginning of happy marriage – no is the end of marriage."
>
> Unknown Author

It's a good thing to know what you want. Don't worry about what other people want for your life - your friends, family, or coworkers. This is your life – it's about what you want!

Now having said that, I do not mean you should be selfish. As Jim Rohn says:

> *"The greatest gift you can give another person is to develop yourself and become a better person!"*

And doing that requires you to really decide what you want and go for it. Not at the expense of others, but at the service of others. Go out and make more money for your family. Do it for your friends. Do it so you can donate more to charity. Do it for the community. Do it for the country. Do it for the world. But first of all, do it for you. Do it because it really is what you want.

Don't let other people's beliefs and opinions hold you back from going for what you want.

Do you know the number one reason why people fail? Because they listen to negative people.

It's the number one reason! You have two options to solve this problem. One, avoid all negative people (this can be hard if you have an office job filled with negative people). Two, STOP LISTENING to negative people. This takes a lot of practice.

Did you know that your income is going to be very close to the average of the six people you spend the most time with?

If you want to improve your income and your status in life, you must carefully examine the relationships in your life and see how the influence of others is affecting you.

One way to reinforce your habit of not listening to negative people is to start hanging around with positive people – people who know what they want and where they are going.

Join a networking group. Join a mastermind group. Join a group where you can be part of something bigger than yourself, something greater than talking about the weather or the price of gas.

I recommend creating your own mastermind group, a group of people that will work together to help each other succeed in their businesses and in their lives. If you don't have a group of people to share new ideas with, get honest feedback, support you in tough times, and keep you on task during easy times then you are likely to fall into the quiet march to death.

You can join our Facebook mastermind group for free to connect with other entrepreneurs and like-minded people who want to achieve true financial freedom and success in life: http://on.fb.me/Tsk8ss

CHAPTER 6
WORK ON YOU, NOT IT

H ave you ever heard someone say things like, "They did this to me" or "I never had a chance".

You see, the average person thinks that the world has conspired to keep them stuck where they are. And they actually BELIEVE it. That's why they are stuck!

Successful people know that they are in control of their own life. They understand that everything that happens to you is a result of your thoughts, feelings and actions.

Successful people take responsibility for their life – all of it, the good and the bad. Until you take responsibility for your lousy income or your lousy relationships, you are powerless. There is no power in being a victim. Power only comes from taking responsibility.

It's the reverse of the Spiderman mantra, "With great power comes great responsibility." That may be true. But even more relevant to you on your path to become successful is that with great responsibility comes great power. The moment you decide to take responsibility for *everything* that has happened in your life is the moment your life will change forever.

As Jim Rohn says:

> **"Learn to work harder on yourself than you do on your job."**

If you are not working to improve yourself then I guarantee that no one else is either. But, if you do work hard on improving yourself and taking responsibility, you will find hundreds of people will want to help you succeed.

For example, I have been selling for years and when I started I was very shy. If I did end up talking to someone, instead of asking them questions and listening, I would just go on and on about my product and lecture until their ears fell off. I was awful at sales.

None of my customers, friends, or prospects wanted to help me out and I never got any referrals. But when I began to really study sales and improve myself and get better, I started getting referrals on a regular basis.

I found people that didn't even want my product but wanted me to succeed and so would send me referrals and people to talk to about my product.

When you work hard on yourself and improve, you will find that the whole world will conspire to make sure you succeed. You will find people that you don't even know or don't know very well who will want to help you on your way to success.

But if you are negative, cynical or no fun to be around then people will avoid you and the whole world will conspire against you to make sure you don't succeed!

If you are feeling stuck in life like you have no control, take some time to carefully reflect on your life and realize this:

> *"For things to change,*
> *you have to change."*
>
> Jim Rohn

If you want to get unstuck, you have to change.

If you want to get rich, you have to change.

If you want to be happy, you have to change.

Don't try to change the world. Don't try to change your family. Don't try to change your spouse, your relatives, or your neighbors. Focus on yourself.

What can you do today that will make a difference in how your life turns out?

> *"Any idea that is held in the mind that is either feared or revered will begin at once to clothe itself in the most convenient and appropriate physical forms available."*
>
> Andrew Carnegie

What did Carnegie mean? He meant that if you focus on an idea (to become successful in business, for example) and you REALLY revere that idea, you really care about it, you believe in it... then all of a sudden it will start to happen.

When you stop TRYING to be successful and start doing successful activities, you'll be amazed how fast things can change.

CHAPTER 7
THE MAGIC OF BEGINNING

> *"To realize one's destiny*
> *is one's only obligation"*
>
> Paulo Coelho, The Alchemist

Begin it! I remember when I recommitted myself to a regular exercise program. It was in May 2009, after I graduated from college. I went running one day and it was hard. After just 10 minutes, I felt like giving up, stopping to just walk for a little bit and not running so hard.

But I stuck with it and kept running. After about 20 minutes, something happened. I had this rush of energy. It was easy to keep running, even though just 10 minutes earlier I thought I couldn't do it.

It turns out that after about 20 minutes of exercise, your body starts pumping out endorphins which give you more energy, calmness, alertness and make you happy. You get into a state called "flow" where everything is easy and fun and time seems to stand still. This is where real performance is achieved.

But to get to flow you have to begin! And then you have to push through that awkward, difficult first 20 minutes or so until you get to the good stuff.

Most people don't exercise because they won't get up and go to the gym or put their running shoes on. But people that go to the gym or put their running shoes on tend to exercise.

Wow! Is it really that easy? Can I really get fit just by beginning? Just put your running shoes on and begin it! Trust me, it will get easier and easier. Once you put your running shoes on, it's all downhill from there.

You'll Never Know How Good You Are Until You Do It

In my eighth grade art class, my teacher forced me to draw gourds and squashes with color pencils. I didn't want to, but it was the assignment in class and I wanted to get good grades.

Once I started, I found that it was surprisingly kind of fun. I got into the flow. When I was done, I had actually created an amazing piece of art. My parents still have that picture hanging on the wall in their living room.

One day shortly after, someone offered me hundreds of dollars to sell it to them. My parents wouldn't sell it because they treasured it. But they offered to have me draw another picture and sell that.

As a teenager though, I was stubborn and foolhardy. I refused the offer to draw art for money. I thought "I'm not an artist! I'm not going to waste my time with that!" and I never even BEGAN to draw another picture!

I told myself I didn't want to. I told myself it wasn't worth the money. I told myself I could never draw something that good again. Have you ever had an incredible opportunity like this and talked yourself out of it?

By the way, this truly was an incredible opportunity. At the age of 13, I was being offered $250 to draw a picture of a gourd that took about 60 minutes to draw. Who knows how far I could have taken that business? But I didn't even start it!

Don't make the same mistakes I made! If you have an opportunity, take it. You'll never know how good you are until you do it.

To master the art of living, you must master the art of beginning. One successful businessman told me that when he committed to an exercise plan he decided that every day before work he would get up, get dressed, and drive to the gym with all his workout clothes on.

Once he got to the gym, he could decide if he wanted to work out or not. But he committed to going. Guess what, by the time he got to the gym all dressed, he was ready to go and work out. He never had to worry about whether he would get in his workouts or not because he committed to beginning. He committed to taking the first step.

The first step is the most important. And after you take the first step, the second step is the most important. And after you take the second step, the third step is the most important. Obvious, huh? Then why do we focus on step number 7,532 on getting rich when all we need to do to get rich is focus on step #1 – beginning?

Worry about the step 7,532 when you get there. Right now, just focus on your next step. That's all that matters. Because I guarantee if you don't take the next step, you will never get to step 7,532. Or even step 2.

Time for Action!

What's your dream? What do you want to achieve? What would you like to accomplish? Write it down and begin RIGHT NOW to take action to make it real, no matter how small or insignificant that action may seem.

Get in the habit of taking the first step. It's the best habit you'll ever have.

CHAPTER 8
DISCIPLINE: THE DIRTY WORD

What drives some people to begin and others to never even try? **Discipline.**

Discipline is the ability to get yourself to begin.

Discipline is the ability to do something even though at the time you don't feel like it.

Discipline is when you act because you know there is something more important than being comfortable.

Discipline allows you to do something even though you're scared as hell of doing it.

Discipline is a habit.

Discipline is what separates the successful and the great from the unsuccessful and the ordinary.

WHY DEVELOP DISCIPLINE?

When you develop discipline in your life and finally begin doing all the things you know you should have been doing all along, your life will change forever.

You will find yourself happier, stronger, wiser, and living a life with more meaning and purpose. You will find that your actions affect others in your life and have ripples that continue on toward infinity and return back to you what you put out.

When you develop discipline, you begin playing big. You become a powerful, positive influence in the world.

Why is discipline so hard? Why is it hard to do what we know we should do? Why does it seem hard to succeed sometimes? Fear.

It's our fear that holds us back from the life we want to live...

> *"Our deepest fear is not that we are inadequate. Our deepest fear is that we are powerful beyond measure. It is our light, not our darkness that most frightens us.*
>
> *We ask ourselves, Who am I to be brilliant, gorgeous, talented, fabulous?*
>
> *Actually, who are you not to be? You are a child of God.*

> *Your playing small does not serve the world.*
> *There is nothing enlightened about shrinking*
> *so that other people won't feel insecure*
> *around you.*
>
> *We are all meant to shine, as children do.*
>
> *We were born to make manifest the glory of*
> *God that is within us.*
>
> *It's not just in some of us; it's in everyone.*
>
> *And as we let our own light shine, we*
> *unconsciously give other people permission to*
> *do the same.*
>
> *As we are liberated from our own fear, our*
> *presence automatically liberates others."*
>
> Marianne Williamson

The most incredible part of being successful and developing discipline is how your "presence automatically liberates others." You see, when you stop trying to change the world and everyone you know and focus on yourself, you will become so influential in life that you will literally have the power to change the world. It's one of life's great ironies that you cannot make a difference in another's life without first making a difference in your own.

Start today.

Focus on your discipline. Write down what you want to do, what you need to do to accomplish your goals, and begin today to get it done.

Self-Mastery

Discipline is a part of self-mastery.

Self-mastery allows you to do the things that failures won't do.

Your greatest obstacle in life doesn't lie outside of you – it lies within you. What's holding you back from getting rich has nothing to do with the economy or your education or anything outside of yourself – it's your own fear, self-doubts, negative thoughts, bad habits and self-sabotage that keep you from living the life you want.

Focus on self-mastery. Become an "enlightened warrior." An enlightened warrior is one who conquers oneself.

When you've mastered yourself, there is nothing else to worry about. Everything else is easy.

What's Easy To Do Is Easy Not To Do

Jeff Roberti, one of the most successful network marketers ever, often says:

> *"What's easy to do*
> *is just as easy not to do."*

It's easy to wake up early and exercise. It's easy to plan your day by writing down the 6 most important things to do. It's easy to save at least 10% of your money and invest it wisely. It's easy to be rich.

The problem is that it's also easy not to do the activities that will get you where you want to go. Your challenge then is to do the easy activities starting today.

Today is the only day that matters. Get rid of your tomorrows and somedays and start today. If you found one good idea in this book, put it to use today. Set your goals. Write down your plan for tomorrow. Get that book. Go to that seminar. Do it today!

It's funny how people say, "They're just rich because they're lucky. Look how easy it is for them."

The truth is, it's easy for all of us. Last time I tried, it was pretty easy to buy a book and read it. It was pretty easy to sign up for a seminar and attend it. It was easy to get up early and go running. It was easy to write down my plan for the day and make the calls I had to make, to write 1,000 words in my book and to succeed.

It's easy!

But don't let that fool you – it still takes discipline. Every day. Discipline is not a one-time thing. It's an ongoing process of doing what you know you should do and doing your best.

Tom Hopkins wrote in his book How to master the art of selling one of the most powerful rules for achieving success and riches:

> *"You must spend every moment doing the most productive thing you can do."*

How do you do that? You must consciously choose to do the most productive thing you can.

Plan it out, write it down, and get to work. If you really accept this way of life, you will no longer find any need to watch TV, waste time or to feel sorry for yourself. You'll be too busy having fun being a successful, happy and rich person.

CHAPTER 9
FINANCIAL INDEPENDENCE

Financial independence is freedom. It is the ability to do what you want, when you want, without worrying about paying your bills or having to work to continue to support yourself and your family. Financial independence is both a state of mind and a reality based upon your financial situation.

To be financially independent, your *passive* income (cash inflows) must exceed your expenses (cash outflows).

The key word here is passive. Passive income means that you do not have to work to continue to bring in that income. A typical job, for example, is *not* passive income because if you don't go to work, the money doesn't come home. Passive income can come from a number of places including but not limited to real estate, businesses, investments, royalties, the internet and licensing agreements.

WHY IS PASSIVE INCOME IMPORTANT?

Passive income means that you do not have to work to continue to bring in income. With enough passive income, you could literally sit on the beach and party the rest of your life and not worry about money ever again.

Now, that is a bit of an exaggeration because there's always some management you will have to do with any business or passive income source. If one of your passive income sources is real estate, you're going to have to manage your real estate properties (or at least check on the person who you've hired to manage them for you).

There's always going to be SOME work to do if you want to MAINTAIN and grow your income. But it doesn't have to be much. For example, one of my businesses I just check a report for once a month and let everyone else do their job. I pay attention to the industry and what's going on and let my team do all the work. It's kind of nice only having to do 15 minutes of work a month on that business.

I certainly don't believe you should stop working entirely and no longer continue to provide service to the world. But the point is that passive income can give you freedom and an abundance of opportunities that do not exist if you are stuck in a financial situation where you MUST work 40, 60, 80, 100 hours a week just to keep food on the table and a roof over your head.

Let's look at Bill Gates for example. He runs the largest charity in the world, the Bill & Melinda Gates Foundation (with a $38.7 billion endowment in 2007). His financial independence has given him the ability not just to contribute billions of dollars to charity, but to actively play a role in how that money is used and to visit schools, and lecture all over the world on how to make a difference in the world. If he was stuck in a job, he would not be able to contribute so much time, let alone money, to help improve the world.

Not only is it in you and your family's best interest to be financially independent, it is in the country and the world's best interest. If you become financially independent, you will be able to use your God given talents and abilities to make a bigger difference in the world. You will be able to serve more people.

Financial independence gives you the time and the resources to truly make a difference with your life instead of just trying to get by. True abundance comes when you have financial independence - and the entire world benefits.

CHAPTER 10
THE WORLD NEEDS YOU TO BE RICH!

L et's look at my country: In the United States of America, we are under financial pressures that will soon become so burdensome, our government will no longer be able to pay its bills and many of our citizens will be bankrupt.

Why? Let's look at some of the factors pressing down on the American economy and Americans in general.

THE SOCIAL SECURITY SECURITY CRISIS

It is predicted that by 2016 the costs of social security (expenses) will exceed the taxes (income) and at that point the Social Security trust fund will begin to shrink.

The entire Social Security trust fund will be depleted by 2037 – there will be no money left to pay for Social Security.

Many other books have been written on this subject (see *"Why We Want You To Be Rich* by Robert Kiyosaki & Donald Trump) so I won't go into more detail here.

But the point is clear: We can no longer rely on Social Security or the government to take care of us after age 65. If you want security, fun, and freedom after age 65, you must provide that for yourself.

The problem is that even today only 5% of Americans are financially independent by age 65!

That means 95% are going to be left living a life of financial stress and burden after age 65 instead of living a really fulfilling life of fun, happiness and service.

These 95% of Americans need your help – they need you to be rich. Not so you can pay more taxes and help Social Security. They need you to be rich so you can teach them how to be rich. They need good role models. They need education. They need advice. They need a mentor. You can help make a difference in their lives.

But you can't do that until you begin to make a difference in your own life and get rich!

THE CHRONIC DISEASE CRISIS

American citizens suffer from the highest rates in the world of obesity, diabetes, cancer, heart disease, stroke, Alzheimer's and many other chronic diseases.

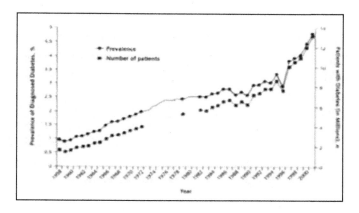

One in three people born in the United States in 2000 are projected to develop diabetes by age 30 – and that's up to 50% for African Americans and Latinos.

A person just diagnosed with diabetes has medical expenditures that are $4,174 higher than an identical person without diabetes. On average, each additional year with diabetes increases annual medical expenditures by $158 above and beyond increases in medical expenditures due to aging. Diabetes increases medical expenditures at any age, and the cumulative effect grows over time.

The American population is about 304 million right now. If 1/3 of Americans develop diabetes, as they will if people don't learn how to prevent and reverse diabetes by eating a plant food diet (See *Engine 2 Diet*, *The China Study*, DVD: *Processed People*), the cost of diabetes will be over $600 billion *annually*.

The cost of diabetes in 2008 was over $217 billion. Where are we going to get an extra $400 billion to pay for that?

And diabetes is just one chronic disease – what about the rising incidence of cancer, heart disease, stroke, autoimmune disorders, allergies, and many other illnesses? All of these combine to create an enormous growing financial burden in the United States.

Diabetes alone could bankrupt our country. What will you do if insurance companies and the government can no longer afford to pay for these medical expenses? Will you be ready?

THE HEALTHCARE SYSTEM

If the state of our health isn't bad enough, our healthcare system is broke too!

It has been broken for a long, long time. I'm not talking about politics here or universal healthcare coverage. I'm talking about the *system* we have of healthcare in our country. We focus on treating diseases when we should focus on *preventing* diseases.

The old saying, "An ounce of prevention is worth a pound of cure" is undoubtedly true. If we spent a fraction of the trillions of dollars we spend each year treating diseases on prevention, our healthcare costs would decrease dramatically.

Eat more plants. Eat fruits and vegetables, whole grains, berries, nuts, legumes, and seeds. These are what make you healthy and prevent disease. Unfortunately, the 95% of Americans who don't care enough to take a good look at their finances, don't care enough to take a good look at their health and may not want to change their eating habits.

So it's up to you to change your own eating habits and become rich.

What does eating have to do with getting rich?

Well, it's my personal philosophy that to get rich and let myself become sick through neglect would be a stupid waste of my life.

I recommend you go for rich and healthy – instead of rich and sick. The choice is up to you.

If you're interested, you can get nutrition guidance and support for free through our newsletter at www.AuthenticHealthCoaching.com

CHAPTER 11
PAY YOURSELF FIRST

This one principle is a key to accumulating and attracting wealth. Ask anyone who is rich. They all know what it means to pay yourself first. The problem is, most Americans do not pay themselves first.

How do I know this?

It's easy. Just look at the savings rate in the chart below. In 2005 and 2006, the savings rate in America was negative 0.4% and negative 1% respectively.

This means that Americans spent more money than they earned. This is how you become poor and stay in debt.

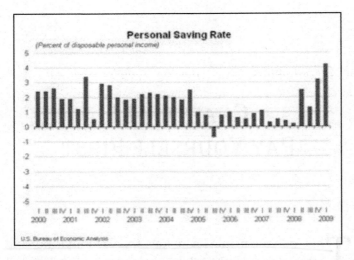

So if your goal is to get broke and stay broke, then all you have to do is spend all your money and don't save any! Easy as pie.

LET'S GET RICH INSTEAD

All successful self-made millionaires followed a similar strategy to accumulate wealth. The strategy was this:

Invest a portion of the money you earn first and then spend the rest.

As you can see, this is the opposite of what Americans in general did in 2005 and 2006 – they spent all the money they earned and then they went and spent some more for good measure. They failed to pay themselves first and invest.

HOW MUCH SHOULD YOU INVEST?

In George Clayson's book, *The Richest Man in Babylon*, he recommends every person invest 10% of their income, and then spend the rest. I think that's an excellent starting place and should be seen as the minimum you will need to become financially independent.

John Templeton, famous investor and billionaire, and his wife promised themselves they would invest 50% of their income and invest it before spending the rest. Eventually, they became so wealthy they were only spending 20% or less of their income and investing the rest. This is how great wealth is created, grown, and sustained.

Now, you might be in a tough place right now financially. Maybe you are in debt, in poverty, or just don't have enough to save 10%.

That's okay – you can still become financially independent if you have the discipline and the will.

Here's what you must do:

> ## PAY YOURSELF FIRST

This means, you must save money *before* you spend it. As soon as you receive income, no matter where that income comes from, save a percentage of it. If you can't do 10%, do 5%, or 1% - just save something!

Make it the first thing you do when you receive income. Today, you can create a brokerage account or savings account (call this account your Financial Independence Account) and automatically deposit a certain amount of money to that account from your checking account every day, week, or month. Make it automatic. Make it simple.

Without money to invest you will miss out on so many opportunities for investing and building passive income. I want you to be able to take advantage of those opportunities instead of letting them slip away!

I've seen too many people who never figured this out and find themselves looking forward to retiring. Then all of a sudden one day they realize they have no money invested. They have no backup plan. They have no secondary source of income (except social security which, as we discussed earlier, will probably go bankrupt sooner than later).

Maybe you find yourself in the situation where you want to retire and have no backup plan. Don't worry. It's never too late to start. Pay yourself first, starting today!

You will be amazed how fast you can accumulate wealth when you make it a habit and focus on wealth rather than spending.

IT'S THE PLAN THAT COUNTS

Most people who hear about this say, "I don't have enough money to save and invest so it doesn't matter." Oh, those poor lost souls.

It's not the amount the counts. It's the plan that counts.

If someone earning $50,000 a year can only afford to save $100 a month, that's great. That's a fine place to start. But if Bill Gates was only saving $100 a month and spent the rest, we would think he was a moron spending hundreds of millions of dollars a month. Same amount of money saved, different plan. So it's not the amount that counts, it's the plan that counts.

In the bible, there is a story called the Widow's Mite (Mark 12:38-44). In this story, Jesus is sitting outside the synagogue treasury and watches as people donate money to the synagogue.

After a while, a poor, old widow comes along and drops in 2 pennies into the treasury. Jesus says, "Wow, she gave more than anyone else!" Jesus is impressed by the widow not because 2 pennies is a lot of money, for surely it is not. He is impressed because the widow gave most, if not all, of what she had. Others surely put more money in absolute value into the treasury, but in relative value, the widow gave the most.

You see, it's the plan that counts, not the amount. If you only earn $2,000 a month, but invest $200, your plan is far superior to someone who earns $20,000 a month and invests $200 a month. Because it's so easy to save $200 out of $20,000 but it takes guts to start saving $200 out of just $2,000.

Another story in the bible, called the Parable of the Talents, recounts a time when Jesus gave 5 talents (an amount of money) to one servant, 2 talents to another, and 1 talent to a third servant. The first 2 servants doubled their money by investing it, while the third servant buried the talent.

When Jesus returned, he asked the servants for an accounting. Jesus highly praised the first two servants who doubled their money, but to the third servant Jesus 'You wicked and slothful servant! You knew that I reap where I have not sown and gather where I scattered no seed? Then you ought to have at least invested my money with the bankers, and at my coming I should have received what was my own with interest.'

Then Jesus took away the third servant's talent and gave it to the first servant who now already had 10 talents. Next, Jesus said something that is incredibly profound:

"To everyone who has will more be given, and he will have an abundance. But from the one who has not, even what he has will be taken away."

I believe this phrase is just as true today. God wants you to be abundant and to prosper, financially and in all areas of your life.

But for those who squander their money and lack abundance, even what they have will be taken away. I have seen this happen again and again. We all know people who have jobs who spend all their money and even get into more debt than they can afford. And then all of a sudden, they get fired, and all they have is taken away – their house, their income, their happiness, their self-esteem. This happens every day and every hour here in America.

Prepare yourself for abundance by paying yourself first - even if it's only 2 pennies. Remember, it's the first step that's the most important.

CHAPTER 12
NEW WORLD, NEW PARADIGM

My friend Glen Bradford had an idea. He liked stocks. He figured he could invest in stocks and make money. He studied, read, travelled, found mentors, asked questions, and kept learning.

By the age of 22, he was managing more than $5 million, some his own, some from other investors who had faith in him and his abilities. That business turned Glen into a millionaire.

If he can do it, you can do it. Trust me, Glen's not that smart, even though he thinks he is. (If you're reading this Glen, I love you!).

THE NEW ECONOMY

The Industrial Revolution started in the 1700s. People used their creative ability to invent new machines and tools that dramatically increased production and productivity in industry.

Millions of people in Western countries moved into cities and got jobs to make a living. In most history books, the industrial revolution was a good thing. It helped improve quality of life for so many people. But if you were one of the people in a job, it really wasn't all that great.

Workers were paid terribly low wages and worked up to 14 hours a day. Most workers lived in dilapidated shanties with barely enough to feed the family. Their lives were hard - very hard - and they were probably worse off than your average homeless person in America today.

There were other signs of problems for people with jobs back then. In 1811, a movement began in Nottingham England after textile workers lost their jobs. Apparently, some jackass thought it would be a good idea to invent a textile machine, which promptly made these laborers' efforts worthless to the textile companies.

This group was called the Luddites. They revolted, burned down textile mills with machines inside, and caused an uproar throughout England.

In 1813, the Luddites lost the war when they were put to trial and many were hanged or banished. The term Luddite today is used to describe "someone opposed to technological change." I would submit that most workers today are Luddites – still opposing technological change instead of embracing it.

In America, there has been a huge debate and uproar about outsourcing jobs overseas to countries like the Philippines and India. Technology has made it possible for an Indian worker with a graduate degree - or several degrees - to perform business functions more effectively and cheaper than an American worker.

Many Luddites today complain about this. They spend time lobbying, writing letters, and yelling at people to try to get their jobs back.

But they missed out on the lesson – that if you have a job, your job is bound to be replaced by technology. That is the nature of the world we live in.

The reason is simple economics. It costs money to pay workers to work. Humans are creative. Business people want to spend less money. So, invariably, someone will lose their job when a person creates a technology that can do the work better, faster or cheaper (such as a textile loom in the 1800s or the internet revolution today which allows someone in India to do work on a computer and send it right back to the US while us Americans are still sleeping).

It took about 60 years between the start of the Industrial Revolution and the time when the textile machines put workers out of their job.

It took less than 10 years since the first large internet service providers started until business process outsourcing eliminated millions of U.S. jobs.

How long will it take for the next huge technological breakthrough to do away with millions of jobs? I'm guessing less than 10 years.

The problem now is that the rate of technological change is so much faster than it was in the Industrial Revolution.

Gordon Moore made famous the idea that the number of transistors in integrated circuits would double every two years. Today, the speed of computers doubles every 2 years or less.

But this problem is also an opportunity! *Always remember to look for the opportunities.* Every problem brings with it an opportunity for those who are looking.

Today unemployment is almost 10%. We are seeing more and more people lose their jobs as the economy goes through the bottom of the boom-bust cycle.

Of course, there will probably be another boom at some point and unemployment will go back down to 4% or 5% in time.

The problem though is that there's no security there. If you have a job, you're at the whim of your employer, of the economy and of numerous other factors outside of your control.

To take control of your life and develop true security, you must develop security within. No company can promise to keep you gainfully employed with a fantastic income for the rest of your life. It's just not possible anymore.

If you look at some of the biggest companies today, Google, Yahoo, Amazon, Starbucks – they didn't exist 22 years ago when I was born. And I can guarantee you that many of the companies that will be biggest in the world in 22 years have not even been created yet.

THE NEW PARADIGM

The world is changing faster today than ever before. This means, that if you want to be rich, you must change faster than ever before. It has been said that there is more information published in a day's issue of the New York Times than someone would have encountered in his entire lifetime in the past.

And you are expected to now learn that information every day. That is, of course, if you want to have financial independence and not be stuck in a job (or laid off, as so many Americans are today).

The problem we have today, though, is too much information, not a lack of information. People are overwhelmed by so many messages and information that is essentially worthless and adds no value to your quality of life.

I call this information *junk information*. All this junk information that we are exposed to just wastes our time – and time is what life is made of. How are you going to get rich if your free time is wasted watching TV?

I remember when 9/11 happened. Some people began watching the news 3, 4, 5 or even more hours a day! And all they heard was negative, destructive and violent stories.

This junk information got stuck in their heads and they became upset, depressed, negative, grumpy, irritable and tired. They fed their brains with junk, and they began to manifest that with negative emotions and behaviors.

The average American watches more than 4 hours of TV a day!

And what do they watch mostly? The most popular TV shows are crap – sensationalist programming with lots of emotion and no substance.

It's actually quite sad – people watch TV and gossip about the TV dramas and they then create drama in their own lives and gossip about that.

All of this is a huge waste of human potential.

Don't let yourself be sucked in. Turn off the TV and step back in to real life. Anyone can get rich working intelligently an extra 4 hours a day – not that you have to work that much more! But it's better than watching TV, in my opinion.

The irony is that today there are more options of things to do than ever before yet people experience more boredom, insecurity, unhappiness, and stress than ever before. Have you noticed that?

I mean, today we can watch any movie ever created, anytime we want, at the click of a mouse – the greatest works of art EVER created in human history. They're there for us 24/7 – but that blessing is also a curse. Because with so many options, we get bored of all the options.

What we need is not a new TV show or a new technology. We need a new paradigm.

According to dictionary.com, a paradigm is: A set of assumptions, concepts, values, and practices that constitutes a way of viewing reality.

What is this new paradigm? Actually, it's not even new. It's quite ancient.

Jesus said, "Ask and you shall receive."

It's that simple. You get out of life what you ask. What are you asking for?

"I bargained with Life for a penny
And Life would pay no more,
However I begged at evening
When I counted my scanty store;
For Life is a just employer,
He gives you what you ask,
But once you have set the wages,
Why, you must bear the task.
I worked for a menial's hire,
Only to learn, dismayed,
That any wage I had asked of Life,
Life would have gladly paid."

Jessie Belle Rittenhouse

CHAPTER 13
TRANSFORM YOUR VIEW OF THE PAST

When I was in 6th grade, my mom was at least 30 minutes late to pick me up from school many times. I got SO angry and upset with her about it. Until I was 19, I could not even confront her about her habit of being late and how angry I got when that happened. Every other word out of my mouth would be the F word.

I realized that what I did was I pretended that her being late meant she didn't love me and she didn't care about me.

Ever since then, I've been living my whole life with the background that no one loves me and no one cares about me. And I pretended that the only way for me to get someone to pay attention to me or to love me is to make myself unhappy.

I know, it sounds stupid. And it is. But I've found that it's part of the human condition. Everyone holds the past against themselves in some way or another. And what ends up happening is that your future has no possibility anymore. It's just the way it is and the more things change, the more they stay the same.

For me, my future had no possibility of being happy. Happiness for me was always a "someday" thing. Like:

When I graduate from high school, then I'll be happy. O wait, that's not it!

When I graduate from college, then I'll be happy. Oh no! That wasn't it.

When I get a girlfriend, then I'll be happy! That didn't work.

When I get more sleep, then I'll be happy! O shit, that isn't it either.

When I make a million dollars, then I'll be happy! Oops, that didn't work either.

No no seriously, if I just get a new car, then I'll really be happy. For real this time. Ohh no - that's not it either!

I don't know about you, but I was so exhausted from this eternal struggle to get somewhere, to get happiness, to get something outside of myself. Now I've realized that there's nowhere to get to. There's nowhere to go. There's nothing to get done.

I am alive right now. And I know that absolutely ANYTHING is possible for myself and my life. Right now. Not someday. Not when I have a million dollars. Right now. Right here. The constraints of the past no longer hold me back.

Now I know I am one in a million in this regard. You know people in your life where the future is predetermined – there is no possibility anymore. You know people who say things like:

"Oh I'll never be rich..."

"No, that's just the way my brother is – he's a jerk and that's never going to change..."

"Oh, the economy's bad that's why I'm broke..."

"The damn Democrats are messing everything up, that's why I'm poor and unhappy..."

"My mom's a bitch and my dad left when I was a kid so that's why I am the way I am..."

Well I've got news for you...

YOU'RE BROKE AND UNHAPPY BECAUSE YOU CHOOSE TO BE!

You see, Donald Trump is not rich because he's smarter than anyone else; he's not rich because he's charming; he's not rich because of any attribute or quality he has.

He's rich because he chooses to be rich.

Any day, Donald Trump can choose not to be rich. The future has unlimited, endless possibilities. Donald Trump could be the poorest man in the world tomorrow. But why would he limit himself that way? Why do you limit yourself that way? You can choose to be rich. Right now.

Yes Donald Trump was given about $200 million from his Dad. But at one point Donald was underwater about $800 million! What does it take to go from negative $800 million back to billionaire? It takes a decision.

Now I know you're probably thinking "Hey, I would choose to be rich if it was that easy, but it's just not."

Well I'm telling you, it is just that easy. The problem is you're stuck in your past, with all your reasons and judgments about why you are not rich now and will never be. You see, if you're still playing the game that your mom didn't love you and you are a failure and rich people are jerks then it's going to be hard for you to create a different future for yourself.

I invented the possibility of being happy, loving, and making a difference in the world. And when I am being happy, loving, and someone who makes a difference in the world, I am rich. Right now. Right here. And it doesn't matter how much money I have in my bank account or my wallet or my brokerage account because I am rich right now.

There's an unlimited abundance of money out there waiting for me to give up my past and receive the abundance. When I am being rich, I feel rich. I think the thoughts of someone who is rich. And I am called to do the actions of the rich.

I complete the tasks which are before me with effectiveness, joy and passion. I no longer procrastinate. I don't put it off. I don't bitch and complain about how hard it is. I just do it. And I have fun doing it.

And if you can't have fun while you're doing it then you're just going to be stuck in that game of always chasing something outside yourself for happiness.

"No, really Tom, if I could just get that promotion at work, then I'd really be happy."

I'm pretty sure you're just kidding yourself.

I invite you to give up your past and all your reasons for not being rich and happy in your life. I know you want more information on how to get rid of the constraints of the past for yourself and create what it is you really want in your life.

That is why I recommend you take the Landmark Forum like I did. I invite you to register online today at landmarkforum.com (they don't pay me to promote them – although I wish they did!).

CHAPTER 14
DOING THINGS IN A CERTAIN WAY

Wallace Wattles says in his famous book *The Science of Getting Rich* that:

> *"You don't get rich by doing certain things. You get rich by doing things in a certain way."*

Now, I know most of you think you could be rich if you were a doctor or a business owner but that's just not true. You do NOT get rich doing certain things (operating on patients or running a business that sells corn flakes) - you get rich by doing things in a certain way.

One person sets up a coffee shop in downtown Seattle and gets poor. Another person sets up a coffee shop across the street called Starbucks and gets rich.

Do you really thing that owning a coffee shop is going to make you rich? Of course not! It's ludicrous to assume that the simple act of owning a coffee shop would lead to fortune and fame.

Owning a coffee shop and doing things in a certain way though - that will make you rich. But the point is this: the coffee shop doesn't matter. YOU matter. It's all in how you do what you do.

Donald Trump got rich in real estate. He bought real estate, invested in real estate, rented real estate, developed real estate and did all kinds of things with real estate. And he got rich. But I'm sure you know someone else who invested in real estate and didn't get rich.

A friend of my parents invested in real estate and, if it weren't for the tax deductions, they would have lost money on it. I know there are others out there who speculated in real estate in California, Florida, or somewhere else and lost millions when the housing market went through a correction in 2008.

So does real estate make you rich? Of course not. You make yourself rich or not – it's up to you. It's all in how you do it.

SO HOW DO YOU DO IT?

Well, I think it's important to understand first of all where you are at and how you *don't* do it. You don't get rich by:

- ➢ Procrastinating
- ➢ Complaining
- ➢ Whining
- ➢ Criticizing
- ➢ Doing what everyone else says
- ➢ Doing what others think you should do
- ➢ Doing what everyone else is doing
- ➢ Settling for less than what you want ("well it's not realistic to think I could make a billion dollar business, so I'll make a business that makes a very small profit")
- ➢ Hesitating
- ➢ Giving in to your fears

If you are not rich, and you are not on the path to being rich and you don't feel rich then I can guarantee that what you are doing is not going to make you rich. Unless you get lucky. But if you just get lucky, you still won't feel rich no matter how much money you get.

Being rich is something that is created. It is created by human beings - by people like you and me. Stop looking for something outside yourself to make you rich.

If the economy gets better you won't get rich. If your company gets better you won't get rich. If your negative relatives get better you won't get rich. If your mom stops annoying you, you won't get rich.

You will ONLY get rich if you create being rich for yourself.

BE – DO – HAVE

Most people don't understand the natural laws of the universe. Most people think they have to get something in order to do something in order to be something.

For example, you might think you have to get smarter by reading books in order to take better actions, like starting a business in order to be rich. Ta-da! You are now rich because you got smarter. That's how it may look on the outside but that's just not how it happens.

How tall will a tree grow? The answer, of course, is as tall as it can!

How rich and happy will a human grow? The answer in most cases is, as rich and happy as is convenient enough so as to not make me give up all the stupid little games I play about how being rich and happy isn't really possible and only special people like Buddha, Jesus, and Warren Buffet can really be happy and rich.

Now the question is why does a tree grow as tall as it can? Because a tree is tall.

That's what a tree is. Trees are always tall. They grow straight up, or sometimes bent or crooked or slanted to get more sunlight. But a tree will grow as close to the sun as it can. Every time. No excuses.

Trees don't say "O, well, you know, I don't want the other trees to make fun of me for being too tall so I'll just hold back a little bit."

But that's exactly what people do!

Now it's true and obvious that certain species of trees grow taller, or straighter or faster than others. But that is just a biological phenomenon. Apple trees never decided that they would be shorter than California redwoods because they didn't want the redwoods to feel bad.

But you decided you would be poorer than someone else because you don't want them to feel bad. Why?

Give it up! You ought to become as rich as you can be. Being rich is not like being tall. There is no biological phenomenon holding you back from being as rich as you want to be. You can be richer than Warren Buffet.

It is possible. When you see that it is possible, you won't hold yourself back anymore. You can give up all your reasons for not being rich.

So here's the formula:

Be – Do – Have

First you must become rich. Really become rich. Right now. Not tomorrow, not in the future,

RIGHT NOW YOU CAN BE RICH. I don't care if you are sleeping on the streets or if you have no home. Right now, wherever you are, you are surrounded by abundance. Unlimited possibilities are all around you.

Right now I am sitting at a friend's house in Chicago and just outside the window is a massive maple tree. There is abundance in that tree. There is greatness in that tree.

When you get present to the world around you, to reality, you will realize that anything is possible.

I am sitting at a table here, looking at the maple tree and the table I am at is made of wood. But the wood table didn't just get here. Someone made the table. Someone created a table out of a tree. This table is a tree. But it is more than a tree. It is a tree plus everything that a human created it to be. The tree was transformed into a table.

You can transform yourself and your life into something completely different than what is there now just as surely as someone transformed a tree into this table I'm sitting at. The only difference is that you are unlimited. There is only so much tree with which to make a table. But there is infinite possibility in your life and you can create anything you want.

But you can't just try to change it. You can't just say, "I'm poor now. I'm going to change by becoming more than I am now. I'm going to get better. Instead of being a weak poor person I'll become a less weak less poor person."

You've got to give it up. You've got to realize that you are not poor now. You have never been poor. You are unlimited and have always been unlimited but you didn't know it because you were pretending you had limits.

Why would I pretend I was not powerful when I am all-powerful?

Because there's a payoff. Because you would rather be right than be rich. You would rather pretend you are happy than really be happy.

How do I know? Because that's exactly what I did most of my life.

See, if you still believe that the economy is the reason you are broke then you will always be broke. Because the economy is never going to solve your problems.

Only you can solve your problems.

"Hey Tom, hold on. I can't solve my problems. My problem is that the economy is bad. I can't fix the economy. Therefore, I can't solve my problem."And you want me to fix it for you? Come on, that's ridiculous.

You've got to realize that your problems are all made up by you. You give power to things outside of yourself, and then you pretend like you didn't give up all that power!

"I'm stuck in the same job I've been in for 20 years. Life is tough."

Is someone holding a gun to your head? Because if not, no one is making you stay there. You're holding yourself back. And you get the payoff.

Maybe the payoff is that you get to avoid responsibility for your failures in life. We all have failures. But to learn from them and move on, you truly have to acknowledge that you are in control.

The most common payoffs people get from self-sabotaging behavior include:

> ➢ You get to be right or make someone wrong.
> ➢ You get to avoid responsibility.
> ➢ You get to dominate someone or avoid domination.

80

Write down in your notebook or journal where in your life you're self-sabotaging – and then commit to giving it up.

CHAPTER 15
SERVICE, SERVICE, SERVICE!

Wealth is Spiritual. God doesn't want you to be poor. God doesn't want you to be unhappy. So why are you? You weren't born that way!

SERVICE CREATES WEALTH, WEALTH CREATES SERVICE

Andrew Carnegie built libraries, Bill and Melinda Gates have improved the healthcare for millions of people through their foundation, and Warren Buffet gave over $37 billion to charity.

What have you done for your community?

I certainly don't mean to belittle you or your charitable contributions and hours of dedicated volunteer work. I mean to show you that if you really want to be of service to humanity and to make a difference in people's lives you can much more service with great wealth than by being poor.

Mother Theresa undoubtedly had a huge impact on the world and contributed to hundreds of thousands of people's lives with her work. And she did that all while maintaining her vow to poverty. She was an angel on earth and truly an incredible human being who we can all learn so much from.

I too have a strong urge to help others but I realize that I can do so by growing my wealth – not by being in poverty.

If you believe that you are serving others by remaining poor and that to become wealthy might be unfair to others, I ask you to consider that with more wealth you can serve more people, not less. You deserve to be wealthy and to be generous with your wealth. And the world is waiting for you to pour out abundance.

From the Upanishads, it says, *"Out of abundance He took abundance and still abundance remains."* When you really start to understand that, you'll realize there is no lack of anything in this world, and that any lack you or I experience is only for a lack of our own ingenuity and creativity.

That is the way the universe works. There is an abundance of all things available to us. If you breathe air into your lungs an abundance of air still remains. If you use love, an abundance of love still remains. If you earn money, an abundance of money still remains. Dispense with the notion that if you have more, others will have less. That's simply not true.

There is only abundance.

CHAPTER 16
KAIZEN

The Japanese have a philosophy which has been applied to work and business called Kaizen. In English, it may be translated as "continuous improvement".

Kaizen seeks to continuously improve our daily actions so as to remove excess waste from our life. In business excess waste could be caused by inefficient manufacturing processes which use too much raw materials. In our personal lives excess waste can be everything from unproductive habits to disempowering thoughts.

The implementation of Kaizen involves making constant, small adjustments in order to improve, tracking results and learning from those results. For example, while writing this book, I realized that it was more important to just write fast and write whatever comes to mind than to try to edit it right away.

TOM CORSON-KNOWLES

This small adjustment, forcing myself to continue writing rather than immediately editing, saved me countless hours of trouble and improved my productivity and enjoyment in writing. Thus, I shed the excess waste of time which I was producing by trying to over-edit and under-write.

Do you find yourself spending too much time talking about the weather or checking emails? Are you thinking about work when you're at home and thinking of home when you're at work? Do you find yourself squandering your productive hours by watching TV or reading doomsday news which is just filling you with negativity? If so, it is time to bring Kaizen to your life.

In fact, it's always time to bring Kaizen into your life! Because it's the same thing as growing. Remember, you're either growing or dying.

Kaizen is not just about financial and business improvement. It's not just about getting better. It's also about emotional, physical, and spiritual improvement. When you spend less time checking email and more time talking face-to-face with people, your results will improve certainly.

But more than that, you will be happier because your life will have more fulfillment because of the interactions with people. When you remove the excess waste in your life you will find an abundance of peace, happiness and success.

DO MORE WITH LESS

I just visited the Museum of Contemporary Art in Chicago yesterday and saw the Buckminster Fuller exhibit. Buckminster Fuller was a visionary. He was a man that accomplished far more than the average man, and he blessed the world with his numerous inventions, ideas, and designs.

Fuller loved to say that the secret to success for a person and for humanity is to:

> **"Do more with less."**

I do not know if Fuller was aware of Kaizen, but he certainly understand that to do more with less you have to remove the excess waste.

You have to think creatively and in new ways in order to do more with less. It's not about doing something better – it's about creating something entirely new to produce breakthrough results.

When Amazon.com came out, many thought the company was a joke. Many believed that there was no way anyone would want to buy their books online and that Amazon could not compete with large bookstores like Borders or Barnes & Nobles.

But Jeff Bezos, the founder of Amazon, knew better. He realized that Amazon could do more with less. Amazon was able to offer many more book titles to its customers, with less cost and less space needed to store the books (since Amazon stored them in just a few warehouses while the bookstores had to carry each title in every single one of their stores which was very inefficient).

To be rich, you must learn to do more with less.

CHAPTER 17
THE MONEY GAME

E arning money is a game. You should treat it that way. Some people treat money like it's the devil. Some people treat money like it's the plague – they get rid of it as fast as they earn it. Some people treat money like it's rare – and they hoard all their cash.

All of these are inappropriate if you want to truly be rich.

The money game is a game that goes on forever. There is no final round. You can always earn more money. The point of the money game is up to you. What would a win be for you in the money game?

Different people have different goals. But about 90% of people have no written goals. They are the poor, those in debt and the ones just getting by.

Rich people have goals because they want to win the money game. Winning is a priority for the rich and because it is a priority they win.

Is money a priority for you?

Look at your life and answer this question honestly. Where does money rank on your priority list?

For me, the top of my list is family and friends. Many of my friends and family members live a long distance from where I do. Therefore, to see them I must have the money to travel and, more importantly, the free time and flexibility to travel when I want to, where I want to and with whom I want to.

Therefore, money is a huge priority for me because money is what allows me to make my top priority stay on the top. Without money and time freedom, I'd be stuck living the average life where I see my family members once every couple of holidays for a day or two before having to go back to a job.

Most people play the money game casually. As Jim Rohn says:

> *"Casualness leads to CASUALTIES."*

If you don't know what you want to get from the money game, chances are you won't get what you want. There's no responsibility and no accountability when you have no goals. The moment you write down a goal – no matter what it is – you now are responsible and accountable for achieving that goal.

You can track your progress and see how you are doing. But if you have no goals, by definition there can be no progress. As Earl Nightingale said in his famous recording *The Strangest Secret*:

> *"Success is the progressive realization of a worthy ideal (goal)."*

If a marathon runner takes another step, we can see that, track it, and we know that he is one step closer to the finish line. He is now doing better than he was before that step. But if someone is running with no goal and no finish line, one more step might as well be one step in the wrong direction. How can we know without a goal and a plan for achievement of that goal?

For example, let's say a woman is working for $50,000 a year. She gets a promotion and now earns $55,000 a year. However, she now has to work extra hours to take care of extra work responsibilities. Is that a good thing? Is she closer to her goal? Is she making progress? Well that depends on what her goal is.

If she has no goal, who cares? She doesn't even know where she's going. She might as well not have gotten the promotion.

But, if she has a goal, the answer becomes clearer. If her goal is to spend more time with the family then this promotion may be a bad thing. Extra responsibilities at work may cut into her family time and reduce her enjoyment of life in general while increasing stress.

If her goal is to start her own business and quit her job, then the promotion is neutral. It really doesn't matter because she wants to quit the job anyway. Maybe she can take the extra $5,000 ($3,000 after taxes) and invest it in her new enterprise.

The point is simple: You need to know where you are going if you want to get there. Otherwise, you may wind up anywhere – broke, unemployed, depressed, homeless or just living a life of mediocrity.

PLAY TO WIN

Most people play not to lose. They are afraid of taking risks.

Rich people play to win. It's an entirely different way of thinking.

If you've ever played sports, then I bet you know EXACTLY what I mean. Sometimes, maybe you or your team played not to lose. Other times you played to win. You know the difference because you've felt it.

Are you playing to win financially or not to lose?

CHAPTER 18
JUST A LITTLE BIT MORE

At Indiana University, I took the Spine Sweat Experience course for the Entrepreneurship program. I had to write a business plan and present it to a board of potential investors.

The investors were very successful entrepreneurs and business professionals. Most of them were multimillionaires and had many years of experience in entrepreneurship and investing.

I worked many long hours on my business plan but I only got a B. I was told by the investors I would have gotten an A, a $3,000 cash prize and tens of thousands of dollars of funding for my business if I had just done two extra things.

Had I just added two little things to my 50-page business plan, I would have made it. It would have taken me only thirty minutes or less to accomplish those two things. But I held back – I knew I should have done those two things but I didn't. I told myself it wasn't that big of a deal. I told myself I was working so hard, why put in that extra effort? It wasn't all that important after all. They were just small details.

But in the end, that decision to not give it my best made all the difference. I will never make that mistake again! That's how I learned this incredible, life-changing lesson:

> *Always do your very best. Not your second best.*
>
> *Don't just "try" to do something. Do your very best and always be willing to go the extra mile in life.*
>
> *That's how you create true success.*
>
> *If you don't want to be stuck with a mediocre, average life, then go the extra mile – that's where all the extra success is, just waiting for you to claim yours.*

I'd do 30 minutes of work for $3,000 cash and guaranteed funding for my business any day – now that I know better.

Have you ever held yourself back by not going the extra mile?

As Brian Tracy says:

> **"There's no traffic in the extra mile."**

I've found that to be true. Go all-out or don't go anywhere.

In business, if you fail to go the extra mile, you will be beaten by someone dumber, uglier and older than you who knows how the real world works. I don't recommend it.

I got a call from an acquaintance of a friend recently. My friend had referred her to me for my business. She left me a message and I called her back the same day. I didn't have to, but I chose to. I make it a habit of returning important calls promptly. (Hint: You should too. People who respond promptly to phone calls are more respected, admired and more likely to earn new business and maintain high quality relationships.)

That woman was so happy I returned her call. She went on and on about how happy she was that I called her back so fast. She said, "You know, most people just don't call you back, or if they do, they take a long time. I really wanted to talk to you and I'm so glad you called me back."

Did I earn that woman's business? You bet! And she has become one of my happiest, most loyal customers.

And all I really did was promptly return her phone call and answer a few questions.

Apparently, many other people were missing out on doing business with this woman simply because they failed to treat her with respect and call her back promptly. Please don't be that foolish.

CHAPTER 19
HEALTH AND WEALTH

Is there a connection between health and wealth? I believe there is.

Without health, you can have all the riches in the world and still be unfulfilled. Don't throw your health away just to get wealth. They go hand in hand in living an incredible life. You must learn to invest in your health and the returns will be so incredible they will dwarf any financial investment you can make.

Let's cover the basic areas of investing in your health.

NUTRITION

Everyone has heard the saying, "You are what you eat." More properly, your body is what you eat. This is just a simple scientific fact that the molecules of your body come from the food you eat, the water you drink and the air you breath.

So let me ask you a question. If you built the Eiffel Tower out of Silly Putty, how would that go?

Of course, the building would tumble down because they putty is not strong enough to hold it together. Likewise, if you feed your body the wrong kind of food, your body will begin to break down and you will age faster, get sicker and die younger.

What are the proper building blocks for a healthy body? Fruits, vegetables, whole grains, nuts, seeds and legumes. The pure, raw, unprocessed plant foods are what you need for vitality and health. They come packed with antioxidants, vitamins, minerals, fiber, and all the other nutrients our bodies need for peak health.

People often ask, "Should I invest in supplements or can I get what I need from my diet alone?" In America today, most doctors, researchers, and scientists agree that you need to eat more fruits and vegetables. Less than 20% of Americans eat 5 servings of fruits and vegetables a day. And the USDA recommends you eat 9 to 13 servings of fruits and vegetables every single day.

Thus, we have a huge gap between what we should eat and what we must eat for ideal health.

To bridge this gap, my family has been eating Juice Plus+ every day for over 8 years. Juice Plus+ is the concentrated fruit and vegetable juice powders from 26 fruits, vegetables, whole grains, and berries.

Juice Plus+ is the most researched brand name nutritional supplement in the world, and the research shows that it helps balance your immune system, improve circulation, reduce risk factors for heart disease, lower homocysteine, reduce oxidative stress, and much more.

The Juice Plus+ Children's Health Study has shown that children and adults who take Juice Plus+ for 1 year are taking less prescription and over the counter medication (55% of children and 42% of adults), need fewer doctor's visits (63% and 49% respectively), and miss less school or work (55% and 51%).

One more supplement that is recommended for most people especially those living farther from the Equator, is Vitamin D3. Vitamin D3 is not actually a vitamin – it is a hormone. Vitamin D mainly comes from your skin metabolizing it from sunlight. Since we wear clothes and rarely go outside in full sun, the vast majority of Americans are severely depleted of vitamin D3. That is why the latest science research shows that we should supplement with 4,000 to 10,000 IU of vitamin D3 every day and get our blood levels checked to make sure they are over 50 ng/mL.

EXERCISE

Everyone knows we need to exercise. So get off your ass and do it!

Go run 3 miles. If you can't, run 1 mile. If you can't, walk a mile. Almost everyone can walk a mile, regardless of how out of shape you are. Get moving.

Don't give me the excuse, "Oh I just don't have enough time to exercise. I can't afford to do it."

You can't afford not to exercise! An extra 30 minutes of exercise a day will prolong your life for at least 10 years. Use those extra 10 years to get the work done you're pretending you have to do right now.

EMOTIONAL

Most people have so little emotional capacity, they seem more like zombies than people. You know the guys who are "so tough" they can't even cry when their parents or close family member dies. You know people who seem to have only one emotion – annoyed. Or others who get upset, break down and cry over the most trivial of circumstances.

To be truly healthy, one must be able to fully express all different kinds of emotions at the proper time. To overreact or not react at all emotionally to the many events of life is to be living at less than your potential. You will miss out on how beautiful life is, and you will miss out on connecting more intimately with those around you.

RELATIONSHIPS

Brian Tracy says that 80% of your happiness (or unhappiness) will come from the relationships in your life. Take care of your relationships. Are you spending enough time with the people that are important in your life? Are you spending too much time in relationships that are dragging you down and holding you back?

Take care not to be swept away by the people in your life. Don't let them pull you in a direction you don't want to go. This is why goals are so important.

You must know where you're going and who you are being in order to choose the right relationships in your life to support you.

THOUGHTS

Your thoughts effect your life and your health. As they say, "thoughts are things." They are incredibly powerful. There are thousands of books out there addressing this issue including Norman Vincent Peale's *The Amazing Results of Positive Thinking.*

To summarize Peale's message, you must focus on thoughts of health, wealth, and happiness and avoid thoughts of disease, poverty and unhappiness. Positive emotions and thoughts have a corresponding positive effect on your physiology.

Use your amazing thoughts and physiology to heal yourself.

ONE MORE REASON TO BE HEALTHY

The average American spends over $8,000 a year on healthcare in the U.S. If you could reduce your healthcare expenses, even just a little bit, imagine what you could do if you invested all that money.

Please note that reducing your healthcare expenses is not about avoiding recommended checkups and treatments. Rather, it is about investing in preventing disease rather than waiting until you have disease to act.

Having regular dental, chiropractic, medical, and other examinations done will actually save you a significant amount of money and illness in the long run.

Let's say you reduce your healthcare expenses by 50% (easily doable if you follow the 5 health tips above). You could invest that extra $4,000 a year and if you only made an 8% return, over 40 years you would have over $1.1 million!

If you started when you graduated from college, you could become a millionaire around the age of 60 without doing anything except investing in your health and investing the savings. Your body, if taken care of properly is truly worth more than a million bucks!

CHAPTER 20
DREAM UP, TEAM UP,
AND COLLECT

Everything starts with a dream. An idea. Once you have that idea, that dream, that burning desire to do something, whether it be to start your own business, become a millionaire or become a sensational public speaker everything changes.

No matter what your dream is, you need a team of skilled, enthusiastic, and helpful people to assist you in making it happen. There is no such thing as a self-made millionaire. Humans are infinitely more powerful together than alone, assuming the right people are on the team.

How do you start a team?

Remember in grade school when kids would get together to play a sport. There would be 2 leaders and they would pick who was on their team. Well, the real world is a lot like that. Except you can pick anyone you can find and contact on the entire planet!

Figure out who you want and ask them to join you. Or, figure out what role you need to fill on the team and then find someone who can fill that role and is someone you feel happy doing business with.

If I could give just one piece of advice though about picking team members I would say avoid all negative people. Negative people can wreck even the most spectacular of businesses. So just avoid them. And if you find yourself in a relationship with one, get out as soon as you can. Life is too short to spend time with people who are only going to bring you down. You want people who will lift you up emotionally, spiritually and financially.

For me personally, it was hard to call people I did not know to ask them for help. I didn't know what I would say. I was afraid they would laugh at me for my ignorance. I was scared.

If you're anything like me, that's probably the way you feel too. Well, get over it. If I can do it, you can do it. And what I've found is that 99% of the people I have called out of the blue have been more than happy to meet with me, answer questions and help me get off on the right track. All I had to do was ask.

As it says in the Bible:

> *"Ask, and it shall be given you;*
>
> *Seek, and ye shall find;*
>
> *Knock, and it shall be opened unto you."*

All you have to do in life is ask for what you want.

Here's the secret to success in life:

> *Be grateful for what you have;*
>
> *Know what you want;*
>
> *Ask for what you want;*
>
> *Do your work in the right way;*
>
> *Receive your success.*

There it is – the secret formula for success! Well, now that you know it, I guess it's not so secret, huh? Good! Then you have no more excuses.

CHAPTER 21
FINANCIAL AWARENESS

Financial professionals miscalculate risk all the time – which is why the financial crisis happened in 2008.

In Benoit Mandelbrot's book, *The (Mis)Behavior of Markets*, he explains what the Efficient Market Hypothesis (EMH) is. The EMH is the hypothesis taught in business school and financial institutions the world over, in most places as if they were telling the truth, the whole truth and nothing but the truth.

According to this theory, Mandelbrot says:

> ➤ "[From 1916 to 2003]... there should be fifty-eight days when the Dow moved more than 3.4 percent; in fact, there were 1,001.

> ➤ [The EMH] Theory predicts six days of index swings beyond 4.5 percent; in fact, there were 366.

> And index swings of more than 7 percent should come once every 300,000 years; in fact, the twentieth century saw forty-eight such days…

> Perhaps our assumptions [of risk] are wrong."

You see, most so-called financial professionals will tell you to invest in mutual funds, hold them for a long time, and wait out the market to maximize your returns and protect yourself from risk.

They claim you should diversify your assets and that mutual funds are a perfect way to do so. However, the data does not support this – not one bit.

Since most financial professionals believe the EMH they dramatically undercalculate the risks of the stock market and of their investments and of the investments they recommend you to buy.

The result is most people follow this faulty advice unprepared and when an event that, according to the EMH, should happen once every 500 years or so happens investors sell in a panic at depressed prices and say "the market is too risky. We better not invest anymore and wait until things get better."

Then, by the time they decide to reinvest again, the market has already more than made up for the huge losses and the investors end up losing more money than they would had they not sold out. Or, in the very huge crashes, like what we saw in 2008, investors lose so much that they cannot hope to regain their losses for several years to come.

The point here is not that investing is so risky that you should not invest. Rather, the point is investing is so risky that you had better know what you are doing or prepare to be wiped out financially. Simply following the latest advice or sticking to a mutual fund with a 5-star rating will not protect you financially.

BUILD A FINANCIAL WALL

Jim Rohn says:

> *"Build a financial wall for yourself and your family that nothing can get through."*

Wow! How amazing would that be!

Not motivated to build a wall? Well let's find out what that wall might help protect your family from.

Have you thought about...

? What will you do if you are injured or for some other reason cannot continue to work?

? What will you do if you or someone in your family develops a very costly disease, such as cancer, heart disease, or stroke?

? What will you do if a major unexpected expense comes up?

? What will you do if the stock market crashes?

? What will you do if the housing market crashes and the value of your home drops?

? What will you do if your employer or business goes bankrupt?

? What will you do if a loved one asks you to come visit them while they are very ill or dying? Will you be able to visit them or will you be stuck financially and otherwise and unable to spend those precious moments with them?

? What will you do starting today that will make a difference in your finances?

WITH CRISIS COMES OPPORTUNITY

There's an old saying, *"It's darkest just before dawn."* Is that true? Well, I don't know. But I do know that after every night comes day. Every time.

In the same way after every crisis comes opportunity. Every time. It's just the way the world works.

Maybe you are in a crisis right now, maybe it seems like night. Maybe you don't see the dawn and the opportunities. That's okay. Let's take a look at what some ordinary people did to take advantage of their opportunities during and after a crisis.

John Templeton invested $100 in 100 companies after a market crash that the world's leading financial experts at the time said were worthless - and 20 years later he became a billionaire.

Most people mistakenly believe that you have to be perfect to be rich. You have to be perfect to be happy. Do you seriously think rich people are perfect?

Look at Donald Trump. Sure, he's a billionaire. I don't know Donald personally but he seems like one of the grumpiest people on the planet. Do you really think Donald Trump is perfect?

Or look at Warren Buffett. This man has been living in the same house for over 40 years. The richest man in the world lives in a smaller, cheaper house than most Americans. I don't know about you, but if I had $60 billion, I wouldn't mind spending a few hundred thousand dollars to upgrade my house. I might get a Jacuzzi or a hot tub or something to pamper myself.

Do you really think Warren Buffet is perfect?

Of course not! It's just a myth that you have to be perfect to be rich. In reality, there is nothing better or special about people who are rich. They simply do things in a different way.

Wendy Campbell is a multimillionaire in the Juice Plus+ Virtual Franchise. I saw her speak in Chicago in June, 2009. You know what she said? She said ANYONE can do what she has done.

She's no better, smarter, nicer, kinder or luckier than anyone else. In fact, if you met Wendy you might be annoyed with her. She talks, and talks, and talks, and talks... She talks loud, she talks often and she says whatever is on her mind. At times, she can be offensive, abrasive and harsh. Even if Wendy likes you, she will probably yell at you as soon as she meets you! I have seen homeless people with more tact than Wendy!

By the way, Wendy grew up with an abusive father and two alcoholic parents.

Is it true that rich people are perfect? Well, look at the people I talked about and look at your own experience. Look at E! or any celebrity gossip magazine or article. Rich people have just the same kinds of problems the rest of us do!

In fact, it seems like they have even more, bigger problems than the rest of us. They're pregnant, then they're cheating on their wives, then they're in a lawsuit, then they're arrested for doing drugs, then they're on probation, then they're depressed, then they're suicidal, then they have an eating disorder, then they shoot a movie and make $10 million, then they're back in rehab, then they find a new lover, then they break up, then they find out they have an STD, on and on and on.....

Please, if you really think you have to be perfect to be rich, you must not be living in the same world I am.

CHAPTER 22
THE BEST THINGS IN LIFE
MUST BE DISCOVERED

I realized today that the best things in life must be discovered. If you truly want to get something amazing out of life you have to discover it for yourself.

If you just buy all the junk they advertise on TV that everyone else knows about you'll have a mediocre life at best. If you buy only the food advertised on TV, you will be unhealthy, sick and die early. If you buy only the investments advertised by the investment firms you will face financial disaster when the next market crash comes if not before.

YOU MUST BE MOVED

They say Jesus was "moved by compassion" for the suffering he found others in. This is why he was a great man. He was moved enough by the drama in others lives that he decided to do something about it. What are you moved by? Are you moved at all?

When you hear of others suffering, how do you react? Do you see others struggling in life? Could you help them in some way? According to T. Harv Eker:

> *"Entrepreneurship is solving problems for people at a profit."*

What problems do you see that you could help solve?

When you are moved enough to drive you into action, that is when you will truly begin striving for riches and greatness. When you are moved enough to solve someone else's problem and forget about your own, then you will begin your journey to greatness. That's all entrepreneurship is.

I didn't work thousands of hours crafting this book just for myself. I did it because I knew I could help you and others solve their financial problems, and because of that I have been rewarded financially beyond what I could have ever imagined.

What problems can you help solve? It doesn't have to be something huge and dramatic. There are countless problems that different individuals have and face every day. All you have to do is help them with one or a few of them to become rich.

But if you truly want to be happy while you build a business, you must be touched. When I heard Wendy Campbell talk about helping others with nutrition, she was touched. She was outraged, sad and hopeful all at once about the state of health of so many Americans.

She was touched by the suffering of young children with diabetes and obesity. She was touched by young parents in their 20s and 30s dying of heart attacks. She was touched by 40 and 50 year olds developing Alzheimer's. She was touched! And today she is a multimillionaire for the many lives she has improved through Juice Plus+ and better nutrition.

Maybe you're skeptical like I was. Maybe you feel apathy towards others' suffering. Maybe you've become jaded and cynical and just don't feel like making a difference. All I can say is, that's a pretty boring and poor way to go about life.

Most rich people don't get up early and stay up late just to make an extra dollar. They get up early and stay up late because they are so touched that they are driven to serve others as best they can.

THE PURSUIT OF HAPPINESS

I recently watched the movie, *The Pursuit of Happyness* based on Chris Gardner's book and real life story of his rise from poverty and homelessness to becoming a multimillionaire. I recommend the movie to everyone both for entertainment and as an example of what is possible for all of us.

What struck me most in the movie was Chris' determination to succeed. He worked so hard, so long and better than others. At one point, he was sleeping in a homeless shelter with his son and he had to be in line before 5pm to get a spot or else he would have to sleep in a subway bathroom.

During this period, he was competing for a brokerage position with 19 other candidates at Dean Witter. The competition mainly hinged upon how much money the candidates could bring in to the firm to sell investments to. This involved cold calling lists of people all day long. Chris had to get his work done with only 2/3 of the time the other interns had.

So what did he do? He worked smarter. Instead of hanging up the phone in between conversations he just clicked the receiver to hang up and dialed the next number so that he could make more calls. He was so motivated.

What inspired me so much about the movie and Chris' story is how hard he tried. He never gave up. Disappointment after disappointment came his way and yet he never gave up. He held on to his dream...

He woke up every single day, 7 days a week and worked, worked, worked for his dreams.

118

Even when his wife left him and his son, he never gave up.

Even when he had $20 left in his bank account, he never gave up.

Even when he had to sleep in a bathroom with his son, he never gave up.

Even when he was disrespected, made fun of, humiliated and scorned, he never gave up.

I wish for you to develop the persistence and determination that will keep you going and keep you working until you reach your dreams. And then you can dream even bigger dreams!

As Jim Rohn says:

> **"If you have enough reasons, you can accomplish anything."**

Chris Gardner had his reasons to succeed. He wanted a better life for his son. He wanted a better life for himself. He wanted more than just a mediocre existence. I do not know Chris personally but if I met him I would sit down and ask him to tell me what his reasons were for doing what he did.

It's not what we can do that holds us back from becoming rich. You see, we can do anything. We can wake up early and stay up late. We can make those

119

extra phone calls. We can run through the streets to get to our next appointment faster. We can read great books and listen to audio programs and watch videos from successful people who want to help us. What we can do is unlimited. What we can do is fantastic.

It's what we settle for that's so disappointing.

Where are you settling in your life? Are you ready to change? If so, how would you change it?

CHAPTER 23
MOTIVATION

The old model of motivation does not work for creative problem solving. Rewarding people with more money, or punishing people based upon a desired outcome only works for mundane, mechanical tasks. Today, thanks to the internet, technology and outsourcing, most of us do not spend time on these mechanical tasks. We get paid to be creative, solve problems and invent new ideas, products and services.

So how do you motivate yourself and others to be creative, solve unique challenges and invent new things?

People need intrinsic motivation for creative tasks not external motivation. This means they need autonomy, mastery and purpose.

Autonomy

When you work with autonomy you are in control. You decide when you wake up, when you start working, who you work with, where you work and how you work. With autonomy, you have the freedom to decide what you will work on.

This is when you will be at your most creative – when you know you can do anything you want to do without reporting to a superior or having to justify yourself.

Autonomy is important because we can only truly express ourselves and our creativity when we feel in control. Mihaly Csikszentmihalyi has written extensively on this subject in his book *Flow* and others. Without autonomy, you will feel trapped, suppressed, and your results will be far short of creative and inspiring.

Human beings have an incredible ability to create autonomy in their life regardless of their circumstances. Viktor Frankel is an excellent example of this. He was imprisoned in a concentration camp, tortured, and lived in horrible conditions for years. Yet he always retained his feeling of autonomy over his own life and especially his thoughts, actions and attitude. Read his book *Man's Search for Meaning* and learn to maintain autonomy no matter what the circumstances of your life.

MASTERY

People naturally want to be good at what they do. We all want to get better at what we do so we can feel good about ourselves. When you are allowed to master what you do you will get better results every time.

You know there are people who get paid millions of dollars to play chess? There are people who get paid millions of dollars to play football. There are people who get paid millions of dollars to take metal from scrap yards and make sculptures.

When people have the creativity and freedom to do something they enjoy they naturally want to get better at it and develop mastery. As they develop mastery they naturally find themselves creating new ideas, new solutions and achieving exceptional results.

PURPOSE

People want to know that what they do makes a difference in the world. People want to be a part of something bigger than themselves.

Everyone wants to contribute to others. It's just human nature. When we embrace this and allow ourselves and others to develop their own sense of purpose and to understand why what we do makes a difference, our results will improve dramatically.

CHAPTER 24
SUCCESS AND FAILURE

"We are not remembered for how many
times we have failed,
but for how many times we succeed.
And we know that how many times
we succeed is in direct proportion
to the number of times we can fail
and try again."

Tom Hopkins

Tom is right on. No one cares about your failures or your disappointments. But if you learn to master yourself, learn from your failures and keep moving toward your vision you will be remembered forever for making a difference in the world. That's how Gandhi did it. That's how you will do it.

Babe Ruth has been hailed by many as the greatest baseball player ever. Is it because he had the most home runs? Yes. But ask yourself this – how did he get the most home runs?

Answer: He had the most strike outs.

You see, Babe Ruth's success was in direct proportion to his ability to fail and in failing to learn and keep playing the game.

Now that you are playing big and playing the money game to win always remember this: You will fail many times.

In failing, though, you must always learn from your mistakes and carry on toward success and greatness.

As Les Brown says:

> *"If life knocks you down,*
> *make sure you land on your back*
> *because if you can look up,*
> *you can get up!"*

Amen!

CHAPTER 25
INTEGRITY: ALWAYS DO WHAT YOU SAY YOU WILL DO

Let me tell you a story of two men with great intentions, Bob and John. Bob has big dreams, huge dreams. He writes his goals down and he plans to be a Billionaire. He tells his wife, "Don't worry about a thing hunny. We're going to be rich!"

He even has all these brilliant business ideas and has several side businesses going. Everyone around thinks Bob really is going to be rich. Look at all the things he's doing! Bob has so much going for him.

He just has one little problem – he doesn't always do what he says he's going to do. He told a big client he'd get their product completed and delivered in 2 weeks but it ended up taking 7 weeks due to a mistake and some procrastination and he lost the contract.

He said he would call on 5 new prospects every day, 5 days a week and he did for the first week but after that he quit calling on new prospects. Bob had great creativity and inspiration but he lacked a certain persistence and commitment.

He always jumped around from one thing to the next. He'd tell people he was going to take his new company to a million dollars in revenue in 6 months flat and 3 months later if you asked him about it he'd say, "Oh that company. No, no, no – that's old news. Let me tell you about this NEW company!" Bob was always on the cutting edge of things.

Everyone seems to like Bob. He's charismatic, energetic and exciting to be around. People just have a problem trusting Bob. Not that he's an unsavory character. Bob's an honest guy. He just doesn't keep his word, that's all.

If Bob tells you he'll be at the wedding it's 50-50. He might show up or he might be off schmoozing with some new business contacts. You never really know with Bob. I guess that's the problem – no one really knows. No one really knows if Bob will keep his commitments.

The successful business people and investors that Bob runs into start to distrust Bob. They don't tell their friends and colleagues about him because they don't want to look bad if he doesn't follow through. Bob doesn't get to hear about the new, incredible business and investment opportunities because Bob isn't thought of well in the business community after all those let-downs.

Oh sure, Bob's a brilliant guy. Heck, he can regale you for hours about the intricacies of a lithium-ion battery and how paradigm-shifting the whole green energy revolution is. Bob even invented this technology that has the potential to change the energy system for the entire world.

It could potentially single-handedly end our reliance on fossil fuels and create a new era of clean, green energy. The problem is Bob has let down his investors too many times.

They just don't trust him anymore after he spent so much of his investors' money on a 5-star vacation to Hawaii and failed to deliver the results he said he would. Bob just can't seem to get that "lucky break" he's always been looking for.

In the end, Bob ended up dead broke. He and his wife had to downsize their homes at age 65 and live off Social Security. Bob never really did manage his money well. He always said he'd save 10% of his income but he just had too much fun taking luxurious vacations or buying new toys and gadgets. Heck, you can't blame him, can you?

John, on the other hand, has modest dreams. He just wants a nice home, a loving family and a good life with his children and grandchildren when he's older. No one really thinks John is going to be rich.

He tells his wife he's going to provide for their family and make sure their children are raised well and have a fantastic life ahead of them. Everyone agrees that John is modest. He's a nice guy, genuine and he always does what he says he will do.

John has some good habits. He always saves at least 10% of his income to invest it and he always makes one phone call every day to connect with a new person or reconnect with an old friend. At work, when John's boss asks him to do a project he always gets it done before the deadline. If he has to stay late or just buckle down and focus all day long he'll do whatever it takes to keep his promise. The funny thing is he also keeps his promises to his family too.

He'll always show up to the kids' soccer games when he says he will. He might do work in the bleachers, but he's there as he said he would be. Some people think he's a little strange – they say things like, "John, why do work that hard? How come you always show up to your kid's soccer games even though half the time you're clearly working?" Some people think John is just naïve – if he knew any better he wouldn't work that hard or keep those promises...

John's boss, on the other hand, just loves him. John eventually becomes the go-to guy for any major projects. Why? Because John will get the job done NO MATTER WHAT HAPPENS!

John always keeps his word, and the boss notices. Even the head honchos in management start to notice when John delivers above and beyond what's expected of him. John starts to get promoted and eventually he becomes the vice president of his company, big company, with lots of growth opportunities. John starts to meet all kinds of successful, wealthy people.

They tell John about new investment opportunities and business partnerships and John gets involved in a few wise investments and businesses. All the successful business people love John – because he always does what he says he will do.

If they ask John to read over their prospectus for an investment and give them feedback, John says he'll do it by Thursday and by Thursday they've got a detailed response from John. They start to tell their friends, and before long, John's swarmed with all kinds of successful people who just can't wait to meet him.

They say, "Tou've got to meet this John guy. He's nice, humble, real smart and he always does what he says he will do." John ends up getting a special private investment in a pre-IPO technology company because everyone is raving about how great a guy he is and the founders wanted him on board.

Twelve years later, at the young age of 42, John's net worth is over $500 Million after his investment in that start up produced an over 30,000% return on his investment. He never set out to be rich - he just wanted a nice home, a loving family, and a good life with his children and grandchildren when he got older.

Every single one of his successful friends agrees – John became so successful because he always did what he said he would do. He always kept his word. Everyone could count on John because they knew that no matter what happened John would follow through. John was dependable, consistent and persistent. That's why he became so successful and so well liked and admired by his colleagues, friends and family.

If you had met both John and Bob at age 25, you probably would have thought Bob would be the successful one. He had already started his own business and was an energetic guy. He was real charismatic too! John, on the other hand, was a real nice guy, but he didn't seem to have any real spark to him. Heck, he just seemed like a regular guy.

The difference between the two that made all the difference was that John always kept his word. He saw his word as his bond. When he committed to something, he always followed through or he let the person know that he had to de-commit when something very important came up. If you want even more success in your life, be like John – always do what you say you will do.

Everything else is just lip service.

CHAPTER 26
MONEY MANAGEMENT

When the subject of managing money comes up, most people think, "I don't have much money, why do I need to learn how to manage it?" The truth of the matter is that if you managed your money better, you'd have more money!

> *"It's not how much you have that counts - it's what you do with what you have that counts."*
>
> Jim Rohn

If you are broke, you can become financially free in a short period of time.

I met a lady recently named Gabriela at the Millionaire Mind Intensive seminar. She moved to the United States from Brazil in 2006 and started cleaning homes to earn a living. Shortly after, her husband left her and she was all alone. She worked as a house maid to pay the bills.

Within 2 short years, she began cleaning homes and large oil refineries in the area because her clients were raving about her. She had so much work she had to hire others to do it for her. Within two years she was earning over $1,000,000 a year!

She became a millionaire in just 2 years after immigrating to the U.S. and she hardly speaks English!

What's your excuse?

Some people think that money isn't important. I mean, it's certainly not as important as your health, love or happiness, is it? This is a very harmful and self-sabotaging belief that most people carry around unconsciously.

Let me ask you a question...

- **?** If you told your wife she wasn't important, would she stick around very long?
- **?** If you told your husband he wasn't important, would he stay with you?
- **?** If you told your friends they weren't important, would they introduce you to more friends?

The answer to these questions is, "OF COURSE NOT!"

Likewise, if you believe money is not important, it won't stick around – it will leave you. And it will never work for you to bring in more and more money.

Financially successful people understand that money IS very important in the areas that money is important in. Have you ever tried to buy a house with a down payment of love and monthly installments of happiness? I don't think bankers would accept that deal.

If you want to buy a house, clothes, food, entertainment, toys, games, trips, electronics, electricity, gas, utilities and other items and invest in businesses and organizations and give to charity you're simply going to need money.

So money is very important – when it comes to buying these things. Love is not as important as money when it comes to buying these things. In your relationships, love is, of course, more important than money. But so what? That's how it should be.

Always remember - money is very important in the areas that money is important in. Let go of any other limiting beliefs around money.

CHAPTER 27
LEAVING A LEGACY

What is it that you want to be known for? Do you want people to remember you because you had a lot of money? Or because you helped people, made a difference, served others and made others feel great about themselves?

One great exercise a mentor of mine shared with me that dramatically impacted my life is to write your own eulogy.

Go ahead and write down what you want people to say about you after you leave this place.

> **?** *When you've accomplished everything you want to accomplish in life, how do you want to be remembered?*
>
> **?** *What will others see as your greatest accomplishments in life?*
>
> **?** *What will others think of how you treated people?*

? *What will they think of your values?*

? *What will they think of your skills?*

? *What will be your legacy?*

YOU DON'T HAVE TO BE PERFECT!

You don't have to be perfect. Not even close. Want proof? Just re-read this book carefully!

I'm sure there are all kinds of typos and formatting errors. Maybe some of the sentences don't even make sense. But so what?

This book will become a #1 best-seller. I guarantee it. How do I know? Well, the truth is I don't REALLY know – but it's my goal.

I've already written other best-selling books so it makes sense that I will be able to do it again following the same system.

That's right, there's a SYSTEM for becoming a best-selling author. Anyone who follows that system has a good chance to become a #1 best-seller. It's not guaranteed – but it's a lot more likely than just trying random things and hoping for success.

Likewise, there's a system for every successful business – a success system or "success-ipe" as my very rich and energetic friend Marco Kozlowski says.

I've created a success-ipe for you – a system that I used to build an online business that earns me thousands of dollars a month and I'd like to share it with you – for free.

Why would I do that? Why would I share my business system with you? Wouldn't that make us competitors?

In the old way of doing business, yes! That would make us competitors. But on the internet – in the new model of business – we become collaborators. Instead of fighting against each other for customers, we can cross-promote, share ideas, and help each other climb the ladder of success together.

You know, no one ever climbed Mount Everest alone – they always had a partner. Likewise, it's a lot easier to climb the ladder of business success with a partner – or many partners is even better!

So I want to share with you what I've learned about starting a business online with less than $100 and turning it into a profitable, fun business that creates ongoing income every single month – whether you're on the beach or at home.

You can learn more at www.BlogBusinessSchool.com – just make sure you enter your email address so that I can start sending you the training videos on how to start your online business and make it successful.

If there's anything else I can do to help you succeed, don't hesitate to contact me personally at tom@juicetom.com

To your success,

Tom Corson-Knowles

ABOUT THE AUTHOR

TOM CORSON-KNOWLES is the #1 Amazon best-selling author of *How to Make Money with Twitter* and *How to Reduce Your Debt Overnight,* among others. He is an entrepreneur and investor living in Kapaa, Hawaii. Tom loves educating and inspiring other entrepreneurs to succeed and live the life of their dreams.

Learn more at: Amazon.com/author/business

OTHER BOOKS BY TOM CORSON-KNOWLES

Systemize, Automate, Delegate: How to Grow a Business While Traveling, on Vacation and Taking Time Off

How To Reduce Your Debt Overnight: A Simple System To Eliminate Credit Card And Consumer Debt

57 Hot Business Marketing Strategies

Secrets of the Six-Figure Author

The Network Marketing Manual: Work From Home And Get Rich In Direct Sales

33 Ways To Raise Your Credit Score

How To Make Money With Twitter

Ninja Book Marketing Strategies

The Kindle Writing Bible: How To Write A Bestselling Nonfiction Book From Start To Finish

The Kindle Publishing Bible: How To Sell More Kindle ebooks On Amazon

The Blog Business Book: How To Start A Blog And Turn It Into A Six Figure Online Business

The Kindle Formatting Bible: How To Format Your Ebook For Kindle Using Microsoft Word

101 Ways To Start A Business For Less Than $1,000

Facebook For Business Owners: Facebook Marketing For Fan Page Owners and Small Businesses

Dr. Corson's Top 5 Nutrition Tips

The Vertical Gardening Guidebook: How To Create Beautiful Vertical Gardens, Container Gardens and Aeroponic Vertical Tower Gardens at Home

CPSIA information can be obtained
at www.ICGtesting.com
Printed in the USA
LVOW04s1056211216

518264LV00010B/705/P